Family Wealth Planning

Estate Planning Guide
For You and Your Family

By Mark R Petersen, J.D.

ISBN: 978-0-359-56908-3

Disclaimer:

This publication is meant for informational purposes only. No legal advice is being given and no attorney-client relationship is created by reading this material. If you are facing legal issues, seek professional legal counsel to get your questions answered.

CLIENT TESTIMONIALS

We selected Mark Petersen to help us with estate law a couple of years ago, and we are very happy with our choice. We interviewed a couple of firms but felt that Mark saw us as people first and clients second. We trusted him then to have our best interests at the forefront of our interchanges, and he has worked on a few other issues for us since. Mark is very timely in getting our work done, and his work is very clean and to the point. We are now dedicated clients and feel fortunate to have Mark representing us. – Fred D.

....

I met with Mark initially to go over my case and to see what my options were. Mark was straight-forward and honest. He gave quotes for legal costs I would be facing, and months later when I pursued my case, he was right in line with what he had previously quoted me. Mark is extremely knowledgeable, professional, and honest, and he explained aspects of the law in a way I clearly understood. I went into the legal matter feeling confident in what would happen. I would strongly recommend Mark Peterson and Snake River Law. – Melanie R.

....

Mark and his staff were fantastic. They were very honest, efficient, and professional. I highly recommend Snake River Law. – Deb S.

....

My encounters working with Mark have been very positive ones. Mark's experience and professionalism are evidenced in his understanding of the law and his ability to develop strategies based on the situation and available information. Integrity and trust are very important characteristics to me, and Mark has proven that he possesses both. I highly recommend Mark and Snake River Law for important matters in need of legal assistance. – Jared B.

Table of Contents

ATTORNEY INTRODUCTION

My name is Mark Petersen
and I am the owner of Snake
River Law PLLC. I briefly
want to share with you my
background and why I strive
to be "different" lawyer.

I went to the University of
Idaho law school with the
ideology that I could make a
difference in people's lives—
that I would serve as a lifelong trusted adviser and
counselor to proactively help my clients plan for
their futures. I believed then and continue to believe
today that a lawyer should be a client's most trusted
adviser and counselor throughout their lives, not
just for life's crises. However, I found that most
often my involvement with a client was a onetime
event of trying keep my clients from stumbling their
way through a litigation nightmare, hoping that at
the end of the road, the clients could salvage some
sort of positive resolution.

If I wanted to accomplish my goal as a trusted, lifelong adviser for my clients, I needed to become a
"different" lawyer. So, what makes me a "different"
lawyer? What have I changed to help me become a
trusted adviser and counselor for my clients?

The first thing that I have done with Snake River
Law is to provide guaranteed flat fees on all estate
planning and business formation and compliance
matters. My clients know up front exactly how

much they will be charged—no hidden costs, no hourly fees, and no bills for telephone calls. My clients can meet, call, or email me and discuss with me any issue or concern without worrying about being billed every 6 minutes at $200.00+/hour.

Second, I have committed myself to providing my clients with top quality estate and business planning to help protect themselves, their families, and their businesses. My clients not only receive carefully drafted planning documents for their specific family but also receive the lifelong follow-up to make sure their planning documents are current. I strive to remain current on estate planning laws and trends along with providing clients with updated legal forms.

How do I make sure my clients planning documents are current? The Snake River Law PLLC VIP Membership program allows me to maintain ongoing relationships with my clients at a minimum annual or monthly cost. What's great about the membership program is that there are no additional charges for changing or updating their plan or business documents—all of this is included in the membership program. Clients in the membership programs are assured a lifelong, positive relationship with me as their trusted advisor and counselor.

Finally, our planning documents focus on more than property and money—our plans also focus on the intellectual, spiritual, and value assets that my clients hold dear to their hearts so that they pass on to their loved ones much more than just money—the process allows them to pass on a portion of their lives and values.

My wife and four children are great assets in my life. The love that I have for them and my desire to protect and care for them is a great inspiration in becoming a "different" lawyer. They have brought me to an understanding that estate and business planning involves so much more than money—it includes providing a foundation of values to support my children throughout their lives. As a "different" lawyer I strive to provide the same service for my clients and their families.

My practice areas include all aspects of estate planning (i.e. will, trusts, powers of attorney, asset protection), small business advising (i.e. LLC, formations, compliance, counseling, coaching, etc.), and adoptions.

WHAT IS AN ESTATE?

An "Estate" is everything you own—your car, home (even if mortgaged), other real estate (i.e. recreational property, rental  properties, empty lots), business interests and ownership, inheritance rights, checking and savings accounts, investments, life insurance, retirement accounts, furniture, personal possessions (ex: jewelry, firearms, heirlooms…even the kitchen sink!).

An Estate is also everything you owe—all your outstanding debt, including your mortgage, vehicles loans, credit cards, etc.

An Estate includes your person and your desires regarding your assets and care (physical and financial) if you ever become incapacitated.

An Estate includes your life experience, history, values, education, knowledge, love, and family.

No matter how large or how modest your assets, everyone has an estate.

WHO NEEDS ESTATE PLANNING?

Anyone with an Estate needs Estate Planning. If you want to ensure that your wishes are carried out, you need estate planning.

Regretfully, we all have one thing in common—we can't take our assets and estate with us when we die. We can't successfully predict how long we will live, and illness and accidents happen to people of all ages. When that happens—*and it is "when" and not "if"*—you will want to control how those things are given to the people or organizations you care most about instead if leaving it to chance.

Estate planning is not just for "retired" people, although people do tend to think about it more as they get older.

Estate planning is not just for "the wealthy," either, although people who have built some wealth do often think more about how to preserve it. Good estate planning often means more to families with modest assets, because they can't afford to lose assets to poor or no planning.

Estate planning is especially important to families with minor children to guarantee that children will be provided for temporally, spiritually, and financially.

Estate planning is for everyone, regardless of your assets or stage in life.

WHAT PERCENTAGE OF PEOPLE PROPERLY PLAN FOR THEIR ESTATES?

The majority Americans fail to plan for their Estates. Most concerning is the 70 percent of American families that fail to provide any planning for their minor children, leaving them exposed to the failed State health and welfare, foster care, and Court systems.

Retired Americans are a little better at planning but often only create basic "will" plans that leave them exposed to probate or other court systems.

Single Americans rarely plan for their estates, leaving their assets exposed with no direction or intent.

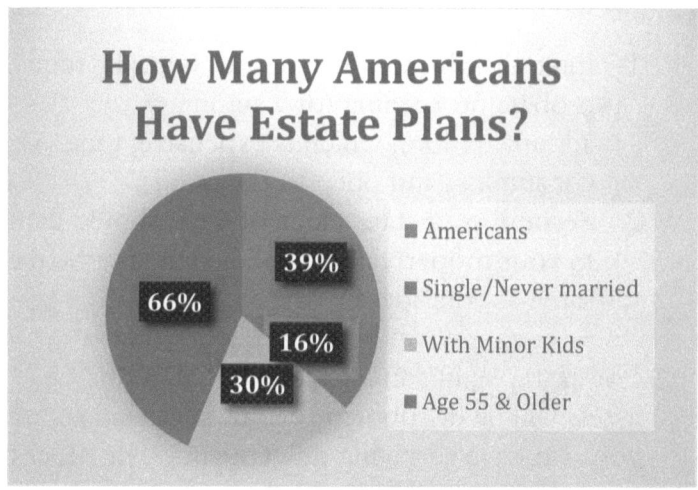

WHAT HAPPENS TO MY ASSETS IF I DON'T HAVE AN ESTATE PLAN?

If you don't have an Estate Plan, you leave your family and estate in the control of attorneys and related state and federal laws. This can result in a large percentage of your estate being consumed by the Court system and attorneys, *i.e. money down the drain*.

Every state has its own intestacy laws regarding those who die with no estate planning documents, wills or trusts, and they vary state by state. Intestacy in general does result in the following issues:

1. First, distribution by intestacy typically requires a probate proceeding (or a summary administration), which is expensive, time consuming, and open to the public.
2. Second, your state's idea of what should happen to your property after you die may not be the same as your ideas.

For example, in some states, only about half of your assets will be distributed to your surviving spouse if you also have surviving descendants. The other half of your estate will be divided among your descendants regardless of their age. This is an outright distribution to minors, which may result in wasting the resources or being exposed to financial predators.

If you don't have a complete estate plan including durable powers of attorney, and you become disabled or incapacitated, a judge will decide who will oversee you and your assets while you're disabled. This process—i.e. guardianship and conservatorship proceedings—almost always involve considerable expense to your family, even if there's no disagreement.

Why work your entire life to protect and provide for yourself and your family; and, in the end, allow the State, Court, and attorneys decide what will happen to your family and assets?

WHAT HAPPENS TO MY CHILDREN IF I DON'T HAVE AN ESTATE PLAN?

If I die and I don't have an estate plan, what happens to my children? Who will be their guardian? Who will control their financial assets? Who will make sure they have the life and opportunities we want for our children?

Without an estate plan, you leave all these questions to the discretion of a Court. Do you really want lawyers and the Court system to decide the fate of your children? My guess is that every parent's answer is a resounding "NO!"

Not having an Estate Plan can result in your children being placed temporarily in state custody (*foster care*)...**and no child should ever be exposed to the foster care system**. It can result in the wrong people (*i.e. people that are good on paper but should not being raising your children*) appointed as your children's guardians. It can result in financial predators and even irresponsible guardians that waste your children's inheritance. The wrong guardians can also limit your children's opportunities, education, development, and even the love and care they need to thrive.

If you have minor kids, don't leave their future to chance. Don't leave their livelihood in the hands of government agencies, attorneys and the Court. Instead, create an Estate Plan with the team at Snake River Law that protects your children, names the rights guardians, and ensures that your children will thrive if anything happens to you.

WHAT IS ESTATE PLANNING?

 Simplistically, Estate Planning is planning for what will happen to your assets and family after you die. But a complete and comprehensive estate plan is so much more.

A complete and comprehensive Estate Plan:

- Passes on your values (religion, education, life experiences, and love for your family) in addition to your assets.
- Instructs your family on how to care for you if you become disabled or incapacitated.
- Protects your minor children through Kids Protection Planning.
- Provides for family members with special needs without impacting government benefits.
- Provides for vulnerable loved ones or ones that need protection from creditors or divorce.
- Provides for business ownership transfer and succession planning.
- Minimizes taxes, court costs, and attorney fees.
- Is an ongoing process to make sure your plan is current and will work when needed.

Because we strive to protect our clients, their families, and their assets, Snake River Law only provides complete, comprehensive Estate Plans.

I WANT TO MAKE A PLAN FOR MY ESTATE AND FAMILY. WHAT DOCUMENTS SHOULD BE PART OF MY ESTATE PLAN?

You want to plan to protect your estate and family. What documents do you need in your Estate Plan? Here are some recommendations, keeping in mind that every estate is unique and may require different solutions:

If you are married or single: A comprehensive and complete estate plan that avoids probate, protects your children, and guarantees that your estate will accomplish your intent and includes:

- A *Revocable Living Trust* that is properly funded and owns of all your assets.
- A *Pour-over Will* that names guardians for minor children and transfers any non-trust assets to the Trust.
- A *Financial Durable Power of Attorney* that appoints an agent to assist you with financial decisions during your life if you are incapacitated.
- A *Medical Durable Power of Attorney* that appoints an agent to assist you with medical decisions during your life if you are incapacitated.
- A *Living Will* that provides direction to your family if you are ever in a persistent vegetative state (coma).
- *Dementia directives* relating to oral feeding to assist your family in making hard decisions easy if you ever have dementia.

- A pre-signed *HIPAA Release* to make sure you have no issues with medical providers and medical records if you are ever unable to sign one yourself.
- A *Funeral Directive* that appoints a representative and outlines your desires upon death.
- A *Personal Property Transfer Memorandum* that allows you to "gift" personal property to specific individuals and get the right property to the right person.

If you have minor children:

- Everything mentioned above plus a complete and detailed *Kids Protection Plan* that **appoints the right short-term and long-term guardians for your children**, creates Medical Powers of Attorney for your children, and provides detailed instructions to the guardians on how you want your children to be raised.

If you own a Business:

- A complete business succession plan that will transfer business interests upon death while also protecting your family.

If you have a special needs child or beneficiary:

- A properly created *Special Needs Trust* that protects your child's or beneficiaries' government benefits while at the same time supplementing these benefits so that child/beneficiary can live a quality life.

If you own Title II Firearms (or want to properly transfer firearm ownership):

- An *NFA Firearms Trust* that allows for the ownership and transfer of Title II Firearms (or other non-Title II firearms) without continual transfer fees and federal government approval.

If you have an IRA account (or a 401(k) or 403(b) account that you will eventually convert and roll over to an IRA account):

- An *IRA Inheritance Trust* so your heirs/beneficiaries receive a lifelong income stream that promotes stability, economy, and innovation.

This list is not all the options that are available, and each person's needs will vary depending on their assets, family, and desires. For example, asset protection may require Irrevocable Trusts, LLC's, or other business entities. Medicaid planning may require Miller Trusts (Income Trusts) or Irrevocable Residence Trusts. A comprehensive, complete Estate Plan at Snake River Law will consider all these alternatives and be structured according to your desires.

The first step in creating your comprehensive estate plan would be to schedule and conduct a Family Wealth Planning Session with Snake River Law. We will educate you on your options and assist you in making an Estate Plan that best fits your needs and desires.

AVOIDING PROBATE IS AN ESSENTIAL PART OF ESTATE PLANNING

What is Probate?
Probate is the
court process to
administer a
deceased person's
estate in the
absence of an

estate plan or if you only have a will. With a few
exceptions, a person's estate, with or without a will,
will have to go through probate to sell assets, access
financial accounts, distribute property to heirs, etc.
Prior to anything being done on an estate, a person
(or entity) must apply to be appointed as the
representative of the estate. Upon approval the
person has authority to act in the deceased person's
name. The representative (typically a family
member) must follow the probate processes and
laws and be subject to the court's supervision either
informally or formally.

That doesn't sound too bad. So what's the big deal
about probate?

Why should I avoid Probate? Here is why you
should do everything possible to avoid probate:
- **Court Costs**. Court costs alone will cost your
  estate $200.00+ just to file the probate,
  depending on your individual state.
- **Time**. Your representative will have to spend a
  significant amount of personal time from work

and family to appear at court hearings and appointments with attorneys.

- **Attorney's Fees**. Most attorneys bill by the hour for probate work at $200.00+/hour. Hourly fee billing attorneys are incentivized to create unnecessary work, inflate their bill, and bill for every moment they spend on your case in thought or action. As a result, a probate attorney fee bill can easily exceed $5,000.00. If you are lucky to find a flat fee billing attorney, you probably would still pay $3,000.00+ for attorney fees. If you are unlucky, your estate may hire an attorney that will take a percentage of the estate as their fee—10, 15 or even 20 percent of the total estate value. Do you really want thousands of your assets going to a probate attorney?
- **Delay**. Probates can take anywhere from 12-36 months for finalization. Meanwhile, the heirs wait for distribution and watch the estate diminish while paying for court costs and attorney fees.
- **Public Record**. Your will, heirs, and entire estate become public record. Anyone can go to the courthouse and access your information. This is especially concerning if your heirs have any hungry creditors looking for a payday.
- **Supervision**. Attorneys and the Court will be supervising your Estate. Do you really want attorneys supervising your assets when they know nothing about you and your family?
- **Litigation and Fighting**. Court brings out the worst in people. Children will fight over pennies. Creditors will stake claims against estate assets. Lawyers will bill, bill, and bill. Families will

disintegrate irreparably. Don't let this happen to you, your family, and your estate.

How can I avoid Probate? Avoiding probate is not complicated.

To avoid probate:

- Create a comprehensive, complete Estate Plan with Snake River Law which will include a Revocable Living Trust and additional asset protection strategies.
- Once created, transfer your assets (all of them!) to the Trust—we do it for you or provide unlimited assistance to make sure the Trust is funded correctly.

It is significantly less expensive to create a detailed, trust-based estate plan with Snake River Law then to subject your family and estate to the costs and expenses of the probate process.

In my opinion, you want to do everything you can to keep you, your family, and your assets out of the Court system.

WHAT ARE DURABLE POWERS OF ATTORNEY AND WHY DO I NEED THEM?

Durable Powers of Attorney ("POA") are an essential part of comprehensive estate plan. A durable power of attorney enables a *trusted person* (spouse, child, or other trusted person) to handle your affairs if you ever become temporarily or permanently mentally incapacitated. The POA gives your agent the authority to act in your name. You can give your agent immediate authority (typically reserved for a spouse) or have "springing" language that requires medically diagnosed mental incapacity before the agent can take any action on your behalf.

What type of POA do I need? There are two types of Durable Powers of Attorney that you need as part of your estate plan: (1) Medical and (2) Financial (sometimes called "General").

Why do the Powers of Attorney Need to be "Durable"? The term durable means that the document (i.e. power of attorney) stays in effect if you become incapacitated and unable to handle matters on your own. If the power of attorney is not "durable," then the power of attorney would automatically end when you become incapacitated.

Why do I need Durable Powers of Attorney? Without Durable POA's, if you ever become mentally incapacitated, your family will be required to file guardianship and conservatorship proceedings with the Court. The Court would then appoint a guardian and conservator for you. The cost of these proceedings is $2,000+ paid out of your pocket or your family's pocket. Plus, instead of you deciding on who should assist you, a Court will appoint someone, maybe even someone that you would not have chosen as your agent.

A Durable Medical POA and Durable Financial POA are essential components to your Estate Plan. Don't let the State, Court, and attorneys decide who should care for your well-being. Make these decisions for yourself to ensure the right people are assisting you if you are ever mentally incapacitated.

Every Snake River Law Estate Plan includes current, updated Durable Powers of Attorney that names the agents you want to assist you. Snake River Law's POA's are detailed and specific; and, the POA's include all current legal requirements, even digital account access privileges.

Snake River Law also includes HIPAA releases and Dementia feeding instructions as part of every Estate Plan, which work jointly with POA's.

WHAT IS A LIVING WILL AND WHY DO I NEED ONE?

 A Living Will is a document that allows you to state your wishes for end-of-life medical care if you are ever in a persistent vegetative state ("coma") and the only thing keeping you alive is artificial life support. If medical professionals have determined that it is unlikely that you would recover from the vegetative state, the Living Will gives your family direction on the treatment you would want. Instead of your family making an incredibly tough decision, a Living Will means that you have already made that decision for them.

Without a Living Will, family members are left to make these decisions on your behalf on their own, which can result in painful disputes and disagreements that could end up in a Court. *Why would anyone want a Court to decide their end-of-life decision?* But this is exactly what could happen without a Living Will. Oh yeah…don't forget that while everyone is fighting about what to do, the hospital expenses are increasing astronomically, not to mention the escalating attorney and Court expenses. Often, this results in your assets being completely drained leaving nothing for your spouse and family.

Remember the Terry Schiavo case in Florida? She was in a persistent vegetative state, and her husband attempted to remove artificial life support. Her family sued to stop the husband from removing the life support. After 7 years and numerous appeals through the federal court system, the life support was withdrawn, and Schiavo died peacefully. The Schiavo case involved 14 appeals and numerous motions, petitions, and hearings in the Florida courts; five suits in federal district court; extensive political intervention at the levels of the Florida state legislature, Governor Jeb Bush, the U.S. Congress, and President George W. Bush; and four denials of certiorari from the Supreme Court of the United States.

This is a prime example of how devastating it can be to a family both emotionally and financially when you don't have a complete, comprehensive Estate Plan. Oh—don't forget that Terry Schiavo was only in her 30's when this occurred. Another example of why estate planning is for everyone regardless of their age.

Don't let this happen to you and your family. Make sure to create a Living Will as part of your comprehensive Estate Plan so your family can celebrate you at the end of your life instead of spending countless time, energy, and financial resources fighting over an end-of-life decision.

Every Snake River Law Estate Plan includes a current, legally compliant, updated Living Will.

HOW DO I PROTECT MY CHILDREN IF SOMETHING HAPPENS TO ME AND MY SPOUSE?

Protecting your children if something happens to you (and your spouse if married) is another essential step in Estate Planning. A lack of Estate Planning may result

in children being placed in foster care or with the wrong guardians. Having just a will may not ensure that your children will be taken care of properly.

Here's what could happen without proper planning for your children:

- Your children could be placed in the care of Child Protective Services, in the arms of strangers, even if you have a will.
- A judge who doesn't know you or your family will decide who will raise your kids, even if it's someone you would never choose.
- Your family could fall into a long, drawn-out custody fight, or there could be a challenge to the guardians you designated.
- Up to 10% of your assets could be lost to court costs and other fees through the probate process. The court process could tie up your assets for years and deprive your kids of the resources they need to live comfortably.
- When your kids turn 18, they get a check for whatever assets are left. There are

unscrupulous people out there who make it their business to look at the public records to find out when 18-year-olds are getting that inheritance check

What do I do to ensure this doesn't happen to my kids? How do I protect them?

Create a comprehensive Kids Protection Plan, which is included in each Snake River Law Estate Plan. A Kids Protection Plan is more than simply naming guardians for your children. It includes:

- Short-term and Long-term appointments of guardians
- Letters to guardians to instruct them on how to care for your children
- Your desired values, knowledge, and experiences that you want provided to your children
- Babysitter emergency instructions to ensure that a babysitter calls the guardians (*practical pointer: instruct any caregiver to* **never** *call law enforcement—this is how child protective services gets involved with your children, and believe me you do not want them involved with your children*)
- Medical power of attorney for your children

Having a comprehensive, Trust based Estate Plan is also essential so that children do not inherit significant sums of money without some structure to control how and when the children will receive that money.

HOW DO I PASS ON MY VALUES AND LIFE EXPERIENCES?

When estate planners talk about Estate Plans, they typically are referring to the transfer of assets. But what about the transfer of values, life experiences, and the love you have for your family?

A complete estate plan will include "Priceless Conversations" where the estate planning will guide you through a series of questions to record your life experiences, values, and love for your family. A parent's voice describing the love he/she has for a child is often more valuable than any amount of money you can leave a child.

Priceless Conversations are one of the Estate Planning options we offer at Snake River Law. We spend the time to know our clients and to create a legacy for their families. When clients include Priceless Conversations with their Estate Plan, we prepare a video recording of our clients describing their lives, values, love, and advice for their families. In our opinion, a Priceless Conversation is invaluable.

HOW OFTEN SHOULD I UPDATE MY ESTATE PLAN?

Old, outdated estate planning documents are one of the main reasons that an estate plan will fail after death. To avoid this, your estate plan should be updated anytime there is a change in your circumstances or desires regarding the terms of your estate plan. **Ideally you will have an annual meeting to review changes or updates.** Having a lifelong relationship with an estate planner that can proactively maintain your estate plan is particularly valuable. If you are worried about ongoing costs to maintain your estate plan, find an estate planner that has a VIP Membership program.

At Snake River Law, we have a VIP Membership program where you pay a low monthly fee in exchange for ongoing access to us, free amendments/changes to your plan, free consultations, free annual meetings, free contract review, and much more.

THE TRUE COSTS OF DIY WILLS OR TRUSTS

I hear this question frequently: Why can't I just use an online will or Trust to save money? Online DIY options can be cheaper than utilizing the services of an estate planner. But remember the adage: *"You get what you pay for."*

Online DIY options typically are generic forms with little to no ability to adapt to your personal situation. As a result, you can end up with a generic document that fails to consider your personal situation.

Online DIY options may be free or minimal cost, but if there are issues with the generic form (i.e. not compliant with state law), you will never know until it is too late. For example, a recent review of an online supplier of estate planning documents resulted in the discovery that a state Living Will form was non-compliant with current state law.

Oftentimes, online wills default to a specific state for the applicable law. Thus, the deceased could die a resident of Idaho, yet his will could state that the laws of California apply. This creates high expenses for the deceased's family as well as potential tax and other problems.

Many errors with do-it-yourself wills occur at the execution point. Most states have specific requirements about how many witnesses must sign the will, whether it must be notarized, and even what color ink is acceptable. Again, without a state-specific expert to consult, a do-it-yourself document may bequeath everything as the deceased intended, yet not meet all the formalities of state law, making the will invalid.

One further issue with do-it-yourself estate planning is that certain assets typically do not pass through a will at all. Savings bonds, certain types of bank accounts, and certificates of deposits usually can be designated to automatically pay-out at death. At Snake River Law we review your entire asset picture and advise you how to title your assets so they pass most easily to the beneficiary.

In most circumstances, it is true that having a DIY Estate Plan is certainly better than having no plan at all, but having a properly prepared Estate Plan can help ensure you reach your estate planning goals while avoiding the hazards of a do-it-yourself plan. The mistakes and errors in online estate planning forms (or in filling out those forms) could cost your estate significantly more than paying for a comprehensive estate plan.

The DIY documents I have reviewed over the years consistently contain significant errors and, when discussing these issues with the person, they typically have no idea about the errors or the potential impact of those errors.

WHAT QUESTIONS SHOULD I ASK AN ESTATE PLANNER?

How do I choose an estate planner that can provide a complete estate plan and meet the needs of my family now and throughout our lives? Here are some questions to ask potential estate planners:

- *Do you offer guaranteed flat rates for their services? Or do they bill on an hourly basis?* Guaranteed flat rates are the only way to go. Remember, hourly fee billing planners are incentivized to perform unnecessary work and pad their bills.

- *Will any work after the initial estate plan be billed by the hour? Will they bill you for phone calls, emails, etc.?* Make sure the flat rate is all inclusive. Avoid hourly fee billing planners.

- *What is included in your estate planning services?* You want a comprehensive, complete plan that protects you, your family, and your assets.

- *What do you do to ensure my children are protected if anything happens to me?* Most planners do nothing. Some do the bare minimum. At Snake River Law we prepare a detailed, comprehensive Kids Protection Plan to protect your children. A Kids Protection Plan ensures your children are not exposed to the court system, law enforcement, foster care, guardian abuse, and/or financial predators.

- *How will you ensure that my estate plan is current and ready if anything happens to me?* The estate planner needs to have systems in place to ensure ongoing contact with you. Snake River Law's VIP membership program is the perfect example of how to maintain a lifelong relationship with your trusted estate planner so your estate plan is always current and functional.

- *How often do you review your estate planning documents to ensure compliance and accuracy with changes to the law?* Some planners use forms from twenty years ago that are not current with the law. At Snake River Law we spend the necessary resources to ensure that our documents are current and valid under the law.

- *How often do they take continuing legal education courses in estate planning?* Planners that only dabble with estate planning on the side make mistakes and fail to keep up with planning options. If the planner spends no or minimal time keeping up with estate planning trends, the "mistake" risk increases significantly. Snake River Law's primary focus is estate planning for our clients. We strive to educated ourselves and keep current on the best planning options for our clients.

- *Do they have an online portal where you can access your documents?* Digital access to your documents wherever and whenever is essential; thus, you have no need to call the lawyer and then get billed for copies.

WHAT ARE SOME COMMON MISTAKES IN ESTATE PLANNING? HOW DO I AVOID THEM?

Here are some common Estate Planning mistakes and solutions to those mistakes:

Mistake	Solution
Not having an Estate Plan	Meet with an estate planner and create a comprehensive, complete estate plan that protects your assets, your family, and does everything possible to avoid Court.
Not keeping your Estate Plan current	Develop a lifelong relationship with a trusted estate planner that has a VIP membership (monthly or annual) program system in place to serve you and your family.
Using DIY Estate Plan online forms	Hire a qualified estate planner. The cost to create a comprehensive estate plan is almost always less expensive, especially when you consider the mistakes and errors often contained in DIY forms.

Paying hourly fees to create or maintain an Estate Plan	Do not pay hourly fees for estate planning! Hire an estate planner that offers guaranteed, full-service flat rates; and, offers a VIP Membership Plan for ongoing maintenance of your Estate Plan.
Not "funding" your Trust (i.e. transferring your assets to your Trust)	Talk with your estate planner about what needs to be transferred to your Trust, and make sure to make the transfers—this is necessary to avoid probate.
Not Planning for Children	Create a Trust-based Estate Plan that includes a full Kids Protection Plan
Transferring property to children without using gift tax exclusions	Properly transfer property to a family member by using your annual or lifetime gift tax exclusion amounts.
Outdated beneficiary designations on life insurance, bank accounts payable on death, 401(k) and 403(b) accounts, IRA accounts, etc.	Review your beneficiary clauses on all payable on death accounts to verify if the clauses correctly reflect your desires.

Outdated Powers of Attorney or Living Will	Make sure your POA's and Living Will are current, have the correct agent named, and are compliant with current state law.
Transferring property for less than market value	Transfer property at its fair market value (established by appraisal or real estate agent);if you transfer property for less than market value, your heirs will likely end up with significant capital gains tax when they sell the property.
Leaving assets directly to minors	Establish a Trust that controls and manages any assets that may be inherited by a child; also establish a Kids Protection Plan so the right guardians help your children and teach them responsible financial management.

Don't let mistakes define your legacy. Instead, create a comprehensive Estate Plan with the team at Snake River Law that eliminates mistakes and ensures that your legacy is passed on to your family according to your desires.

Disclaimer:

This publication is meant for informational purposes only. No legal advice is being given and no attorney-client relationship is created by reading this material. If you are facing legal issues, seek professional legal counsel to get your questions answered.

SNAKE RIVER LAW PLLC (208-406-9885)

1156 E Center St.
Pocatello, ID 83201

www.snakeriverlaw.com

www.ingramcontent.com/pod-product-compliance
Lightning Source LLC
Chambersburg PA
CBHW020956180526
45163CB00006B/2390